TERRY AND THE DINOSAURS

by MIKE & SABRINA RUCKER

Another adventure in the *Terry the Tractor*™ Series

FIRST EDITION

UNIVERSITY EDITIONS, Inc.
c/o Mike Rucker
1003 W. Centennial Dr.
Peoria, IL 61614-2828

Cover and interior art by Bob Burchett

"We learn an awful lot from failures. Failures tell
you what you must not do in the future."
— *Henry Petrosky,*
Civil Engineer

Terry the Tractor® and University Editions™ are trademarks of Michael P. Rucker

The Licensed Trademark of the elevated sprocket design illustrated
is owned and registered by Caterpillar Inc. Used by permission.

Terry the Tractor is a Licensed Trademark of Michael P. Rucker.

Mike dedicates this book to his cousin
Charlotte Williams and her nine grandchildren:
Weston, Lee, Gordon, Turner, Shep,
Lâle, Brice, Charlotte and Levent.

Thanks for editing and proofreading to
Yvonne Frey of Peoria, Illinois and to
Sherry Seckler of Peoria for the music composition.

A track-type tractor in a logging operation is often called a skidder.

Terry and his boss were visiting State University. They had been invited there to talk with Professor Portend about an exciting new project.

They had some extra time so they decided to visit the dinosaur fossil exhibit at the university museum.

"Oh, look!" Terry called out. "That's the fossil skeleton of a Tyrannosaurus rex. Look at its teeth," he said referring to the sharp jagged teeth in that skeleton. "This dinosaur definitely ate meat."

"That's right, Terry, you know something about dinosaurs, don't you? Over here is a stegosaur skeleton. They are easy to identify because they have these plates along their back," the boss said.

"Yes," Terry said and this is an ankylosaurus with a big club on the end of its tail. He would use that to protect himself. He might have even been able to drive a tyrannosaur away."

8

Just then a woman approached them. She introduced herself, "I am Professor Paleo. I study and teach about dinosaurs here at the university. May I show you around?"

"Yes, please do. That must be a very exciting job," Terry said.

"Yes, it is," Professor Paleo answered. "We are finding out lots of new and exciting things about dinosaurs. Did you see the huge diplodocus dinosaur skeleton?" she asked as they looked at the fossil skeleton of a long-necked dinosaur. This dinosaur was a vegetarian. It ate only plants. You can see that its teeth are flat for grinding up plant leaves."

"Its head is so tiny compared to its huge body," Terry commented.

"Yes," the professor answered. "It had a very small brain. In fact, the diplodocus had the smallest brain of any dinosaur if you compared the brain to the size of its body."

"Now, let me show you a new exhibit we just put in the museum."

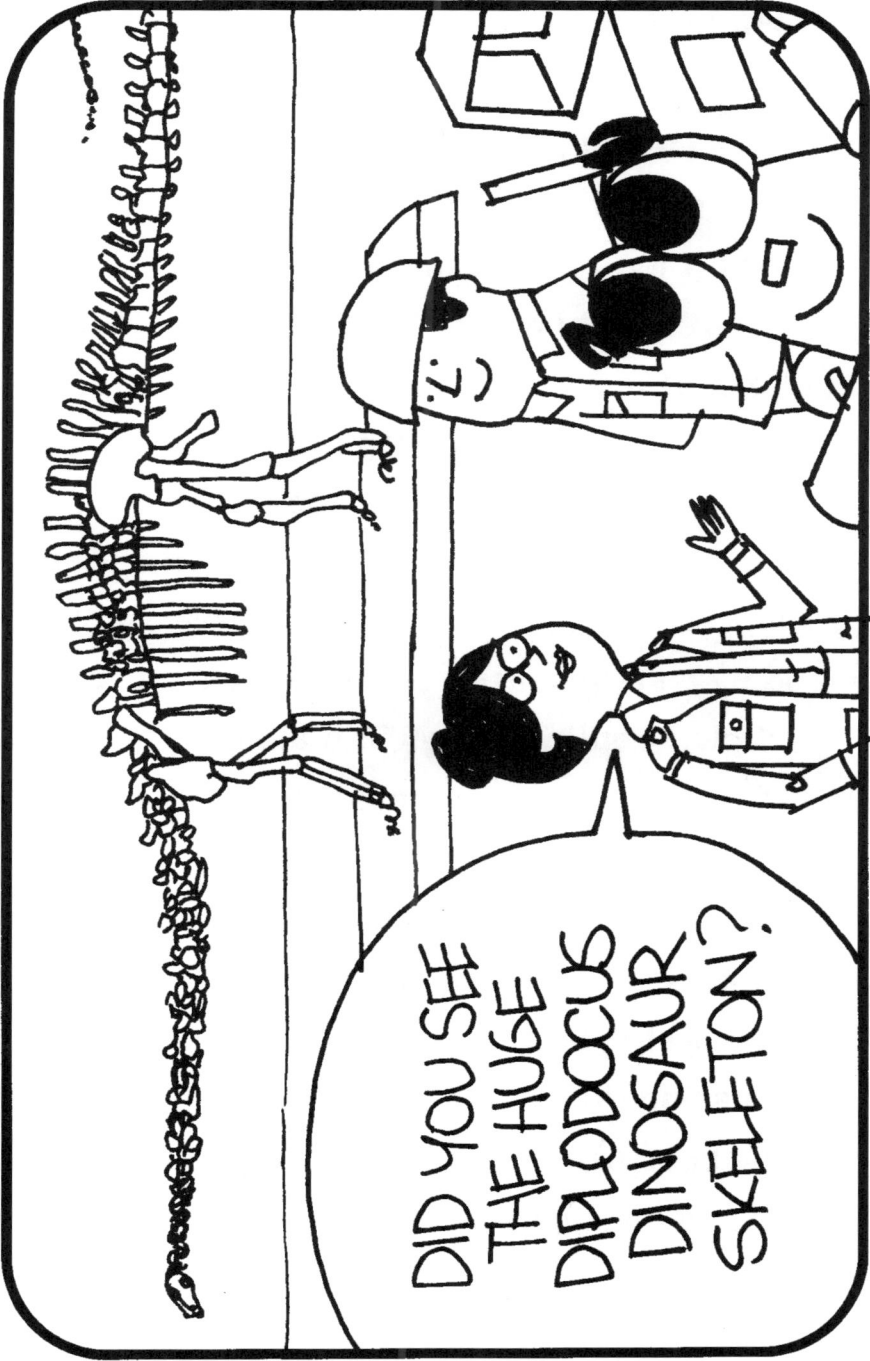

She took them to an exhibit that was placed flat on the floor. She pointed to the exhibit and said, "These are dinosaur tracks. When dinosaurs stepped in soft mud, they left these tracks. Then the mud dried out and turned to fossil."

"What kind of dinosaurs made these tracks?" the boss asked.

"Well," Professor Paleo replied, "Those big round flat ones were made by a diplodocus. The ones with three toes and a big claw on each one were made by a tyrannosaurus. Over here are some that were probably made by a stegosaurus and an ankylosaurus."

"Wow!" replied Terry. "It's amazing that you found actual dinosaur tracks and can even tell what kind of dinosaur made them."

"We are still excavating the site where we found these tracks," the professor told them. "There are many more tracks to yet be uncovered. We are learning new and amazing things about dinosaurs all the time."

The boss said, "This has been a great visit, but we have to go to meet Professor Portend. He wants to talk with Terry about his exciting new project."

So Terry and the boss went to the Physics and Engineering Building where Professor Portend was expecting them.

"Terry, let me introduce you to Professor Portend," the boss said. "I understand that you are working on a project and would like Terry to help with it," he said to the scientist.

"I do indeed have need of Terry's help," said the professor

"Of course," Terry said. "I always like to help."

"Well, it is a very, very interesting project," Professor Portend told him. "I teach the subject of Physical Impossibilities here at the university," said the professor. "I would indeed like your assistance, if you would care to volunteer for it. It may be a bit risky. It's never been attempted before."

"Tell me about it," said Terry. "I like to learn new things."

"I have invented a time capsule. My plan is to send a volunteer 65 million years into the future to see what the world will be like then. And I hope you will agree to be part of this exciting project," Professor Portend told him.

"Why me?" asked Terry. "Why don't you send a human being?"

"This time machine will take the volunteer into the future faster than the speed of light. You will pass through several time warp curtains that we refer to as 'wormholes'."

Terry laughed, "Wormhole! No one can go through a wormhole."

"Well, it's not really an actual wormhole. That's just what we call a path that takes someone – or something – from one dimension to another. And time is a dimension. The wormhole will have several time warp curtains that are extremely hot and extremely cold both at the same time. A human could not survive this, but a machine like you could do it," Professor Portend explained. "Would you consider trying this, Terry?"

"It sounds exciting," said Terry. "I would be willing to go – if you think I will be safe. Do you think I can come back without getting badly damaged – or even stranded in the future?"

"Oh, I'm fairly sure of it," said Professor Portend. "Of course strange things can happen, especially with new technology such as this. But I have taken every possible step to be sure that you will be safe."

The time machine was a big metal box. It had a door on one side that was just large enough for Terry to go inside. There were all sorts of dials and gauges and wires on the sides of the box.

"We made it for a tractor just your size. When you are inside we will close the door and set the machine to go forward in time 65 million years," Professor Portend explained. "We are ready to start the project now. Are you ready to go? What we want you to do is visit the future Earth and come back to tell us everything you learn. This is the most exciting project in history!" the professor said enthusiastically.

"How will I be able to talk with you if I am in the future?" Terry asked.

"You will not be able to communicate with us, because you will be in the future, while we are still here in the present."

"Then, how will I get the time machine to bring me back to the present time," Terry asked.

"An excellent question," Professor Portend said. "All you have to do is come back into the time capsule. The door will close and the machine will automatically bring you back to us today. No time will have passed for us here at the university."

Terry was a bit concerned about his safety, but the project was so exciting that he agreed to do it. "Okay," he exclaimed. "I agree to be the first time traveler in history."

"When you are in the time machine I will set the controls to take you 65 million years into the future," Professor Portend said. "When you get there the door will automatically open and you will be the first person – er – machine, to see what the world will be like many years in the future. Good luck!"

"Well here I go," Terry exclaimed.

Terry went into the time capsule and the door shut behind him. Soon he felt a rush of air and it seemed as if the walls of the time machine had disappeared. It was as if he were flying through space. Then he felt extreme heat – no, or was it cold? He then realized that no human being could stand such extremes of hot and cold, which was why a machine like him had to be the first time traveler.

"Well, at least there are no worms in this wormhole," he laughed.

Soon the rush of the air stopped, and the walls of the time machine slowly reappeared around him. He also felt the motion of the time machine stop. Then the door opened and Terry peered out at the strange surroundings.

23

He had no idea what to expect, but what he saw was an entire surprise. He was in a forest, but it was not like any forest that he had ever seen before. The trees were all different. They looked more like giant ferns than trees. The ground was very wet and swampy with lots of small ferns and plants growing thickly together.

He left the time capsule and began to wander around. "I must remember where the time capsule is so I can find it when I want to go back to the past," thought Terry as he glanced around to locate his landing place. "Where are all the people?" he wondered.

As he wandered away from the time machine he soon came to a large flat area of mud. There were some tracks in the soft mud. Terry thought, "Wow, these are like the dinosaur footprints that Professor Paleo showed me in the museum."

He was still very uncertain as to what to expect, but he went on a bit further. He came to a large lake. In the lake, some distance from the shore, he saw a huge animal. It was standing in the water, but its long neck was high above the water. Terry could also see that it had a long tail.

Terry thought, "That animal looks exactly like a diplodocus. I thought that they only lived in the past, not far into the future where I am supposed to be now."

"Oh no!" Terry wailed as he suddenly realized that the time machine must have sent him 65 million years into the PAST – not into the future.

Soon the diplodocus saw Terry and made its way slowly over to him on the shore. Terry was not afraid of it. He knew it was a vegetarian and not a mean animal. When it came near, Terry decided to see if he could talk to the animal. He called out, "Are you a diplodocus?"

The big animal replied in a very strange accent, "I dun't kno what dot means. Who – an what – are yuu? I never seen you afore."

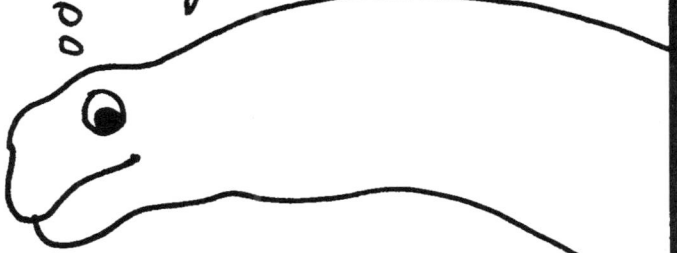

Terry was delighted that he could talk with the animal. "I am a tractor," he answered. "My name is Terry. I am from the past – no, I mean the future. I guess I'm very confused," Terry admitted.

"Dot's okay," said the diplodocus. "I gits confused tuu. Yuu kin call me 'Dippy'," the friendly animal told him as she stepped out of the water. Terry now saw that she was much bigger than he was. Terry was now sure that the animal was indeed a diplodocus.

"Yuu mus' be careful," Dippy told Terry. "Mos' of us here are friendly. But sum are terrible. Dey like to eat us. Dey might try to eat yuu."

"Oh, I don't think that would be a problem," Terry told Dippy. "I'm made of steel. No animal could eat me."

"Dey might try," Dippy warned.

"I'm new here and I don't know my way around. Could you please show me around the area?" Terry asked, trying to change the subject.

"Okey," Dippy answered. "Let's go dis way."

As Terry and Dippy went along together, they came to an open area in the forest. It looked like a big patch of smooth black soil. Terry did not want to cross the black soil, but Dippy went right across it.

As they started across this area, Terry could feel the ground shaking under his tracks like jelly. He was about to say something about it to Dippy when suddenly one of her feet sank deeply into the sticky, black soil. When she tried to pull her foot from the sticky soil her other feet all began to sink.

Terry did not sink because his tracks spread his weight and kept him on top of the ground.

Dippy then knew what the problem was. "Oh, no," she cried. "Dis is a tar pit. I'm sinking into it fast!"

Terry thought, "Well, I knew that diplodocus dinosaurs had a small brain. I guess this proves it. I wonder how I can help her?"

All four feet of the heavy dinosaur were now stuck and her belly was almost touching the black soil. The more she struggled the deeper she sank. "I'm goin ta die!" she cried.

Terry knew that he had to try to save Dippy. He called to her, "Stop struggling. I'm going to try to push you out of the tar pit."

Very slowly and carefully he placed his bulldozer against the belly of his dinosaur friend. Then he began to slowly push her. He was careful not to spin his tracks in the sticky soil. He knew that if his tracks spun he would sink as well.

Slowly and carefully he pushed Dippy to the edge of the tar pit. Finally she was able to find solid ground to stand on and get out of the sticky black dirt.

"Yuu saved mi life," Dippy said when she was finally safe on solid ground. She was still shaking from the experience.

"I'm glad I was able to push you out without sinking into the tar pit myself," Terry told her.

Terry told Dippy, "When I'm happy about something, I like to make up a new song and sing. Here's a song we can sing together.

The two new friends soon were harmonizing this song.

As Terry and Dippy were singing, another huge dinosaur came into view. It had a large club at the end of its tail. Terry recognized it as an ankylosaurus. This animal came towards them munching plants as it came.

When the ankylosaurus saw Terry, he stopped and called out to Dippy, "Who dat be? Du I need hit 'im with mi tail club?"

"No," Dippy answered. "Dis animal be a frien. He saved mi life. He say he be a machin'. He eat plants like yuu an' me."

"I really don't eat plants, but I do want to be your friend," Terry told them both.

"As long as yuu dun' try ta eat me yuu be okey," the ankylosaurus said. "Yuu kin call me 'Anky'."

Soon another dinosaur came within view. It was walking fast towards them. Terry recognized it as a stegosaurus by the big plates on its back. Terry knew that it was also a friendly plant eating animal.

Dippy introduced Terry to the stegosaur, "Terry meet our frien Steggy."

"I'm pleased to meet you," said Terry.

Steggy grunted, "Hullo. I saw dat awful Tyro back dere in de forest. I was a coming this way to git outer his way."

Terry knew that Steggy was probably referring to a Tyrannosaurus rex. He could see that all of the other dinosaurs were afraid of the tyrannosaur as well.

"Den we all better go dis way an stay outer Tyro's path," Anky said.

The other plant eating dinosaurs agreed, so they all started off in the direction away from the tyrannosaur.

But soon the animals and Terry heard trees crashing in the forest behind them. Then they heard the roar of a huge beast. They looked back and saw the tyrannosaur's head towering above the trees. It was coming right towards them – and fast.

Terry and the plant eating dinosaurs began to run as fast as they could. The tyrannosaur was still gaining on them.

Soon the tyrannosaur caught up with them. He tried to take a bite out of Steggy, but Anky was nearby and swung the club on his tail at Tyro. He hit the huge meateater on one of his legs. The tyrannosaur roared in pain and backed off. Terry turned to face their huge enemy.

Terry thought that since he was made of steel that he should try to save the others, because Tyro could kill his new dinosaur friends. Terry rushed towards Tyro and his bulldozer hit Tyro's other leg. The tyrannosaur again roared, but this time he opened his fierce jaws and clamped them down on Terry.

Tyro picked Terry up and tossed him into the
air. Terry landed upside down and could not get up.

Tyro was really mad and fierce looking now. The mean dinosaur decided to finish Terry off. He came after Terry and again bit him. He picked him up into the air and once again swung him around.

Then he dropped Terry. Fortunately Terry landed right side up this time. He was bent up but found that he could still move.

The tyrannosaur was about to come at the others again when something caught the attention of all of the dinosaurs. It was a loud noise in the sky. It was like thunder – only much louder.

Then they saw a brilliant flash in the sky. Terry recognized it as a huge comet or meteor. Within a few seconds it struck the ground some distance from Terry and the others. Soon the ground shook with the force of a great earthquake.

As Terry and the frightened dinosaurs watched they saw a huge black cloud rising in the sky. They soon realized that the black cloud was coming towards them at great speed.

They knew that the cloud meant danger for them all. They realized that it could kill all of them.

Even Tyro forgot that he was hungry. All the dinosaurs, and Terry as well, began running as hard as they could away from the on-rushing black cloud.

The cloud was gaining on them. Fortunately for Terry, they were fleeing towards the place where he had left the time capsule.

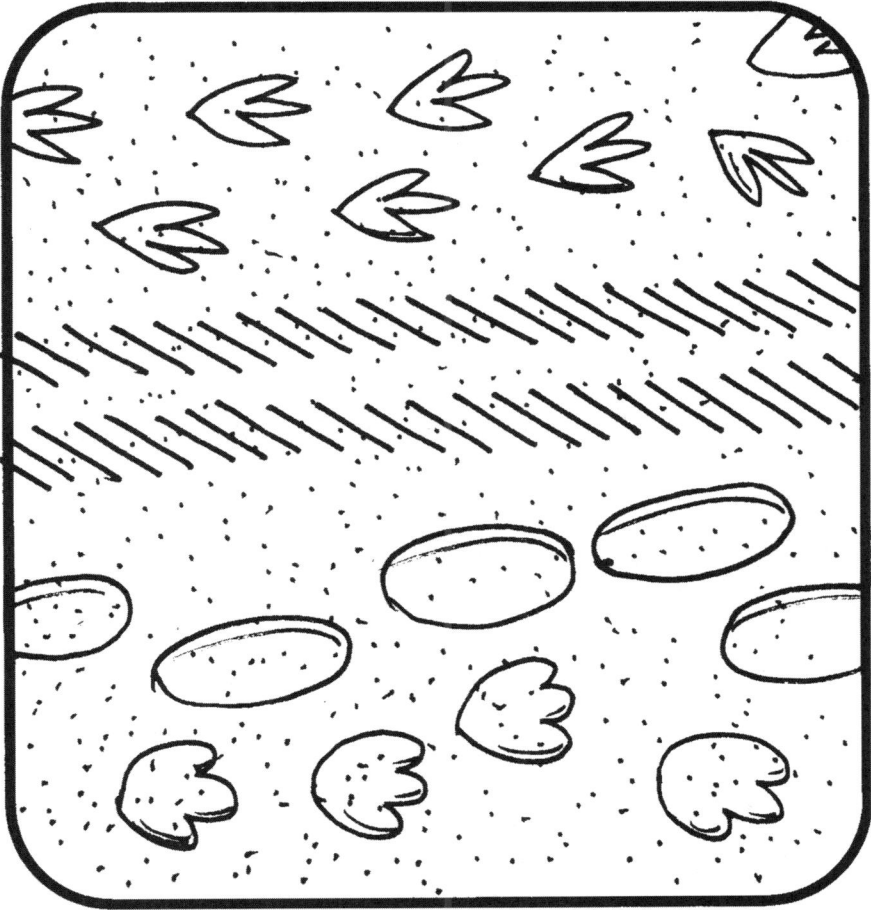

As they ran for their lives they came to the flat expanse of mud. They could run faster across the mud, but the black cloud was still gaining on them. The dinosaurs and Terry made footprints as they crossed the mud.

Terry reached the time capsule with the black cloud coming fast behind him. He dashed into the module. The door quickly shut behind him. He felt terrible that the dinosaurs could not enter the time capsule with him. He knew they would probably all die. Then he felt and heard the rushing of air. Again the walls of the module faded and he felt as if he were flying through space. Down through the time warp wormhole he plunged. Again he experienced the extreme heat and cold that he had felt before.

After a while the walls reappeared and the door to the time capsule opened. Terry exited the machine. There were Professor Precursor and the boss standing right where he had last seen them. In fact, they had not even moved.

"Gosh," said the boss, "the time capsule door was closed less than a minute. Did you go anywhere, Terry? You look so beat up and dirty. What happened?"

"Go anywhere!" said a very tired Terry. "I have been with dinosaurs. And, and, – I had to fight a Tyrannosaurus rex. And, and I had to flee from a giant black cloud that was caused by a comet that struck the Earth. I thought this machine was supposed to take me into the future."

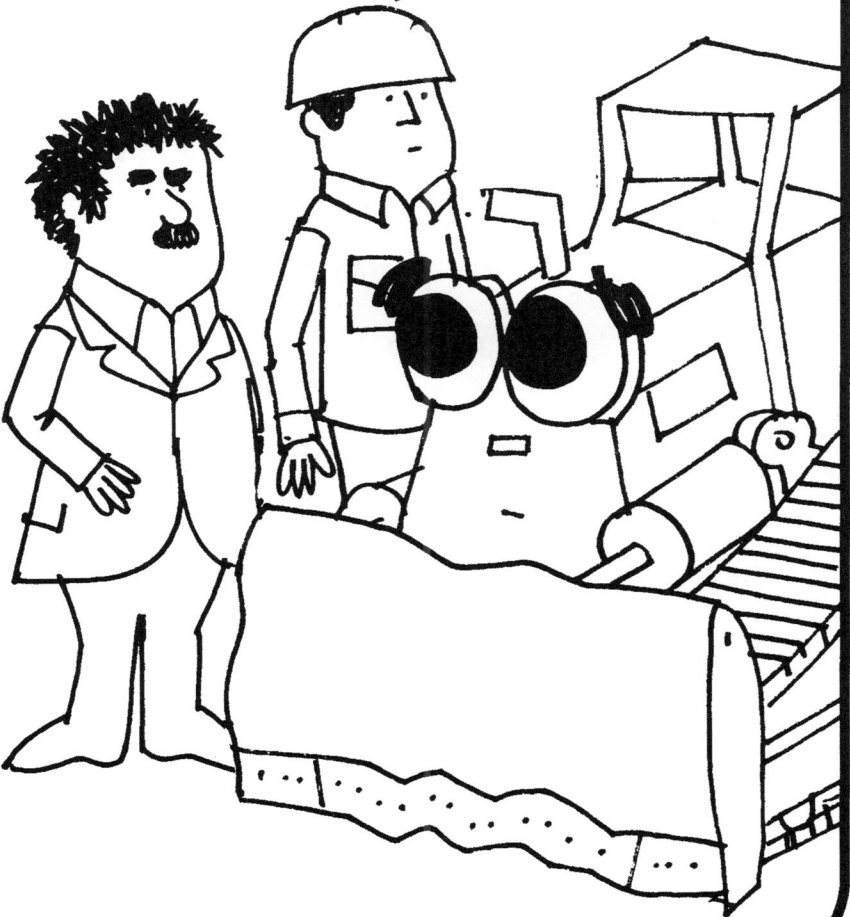

"Well, it was," said Professor Portend. "But apparently it has a problem of some sort. I think it took you 65 million years into the past instead of into the future."

"It sure did!" Terry stated. I almost didn't escape from the black cloud caused by the comet. I think it must have killed all of my dinosaur friends."

"Goodness!" said the professor. "I have a lot of work to do on my machine to get it to work properly. Terry, I want to talk with you about your experience. But now I must work on my machine. Can you come again soon?"

"Of course," said Terry. "Right now I want to go to the workshop to get some of these dents taken out."

Terry and the boss went past the dinosaur museum as they were leaving. As they went along the boss asked him, "Terry, just how did you get all those dents and scrapes?"

"The tyrannosaurus made most of them, I think," Terry replied. He was about to explain more when Professor Paleo saw them and came quickly over.

"Terry, I am so glad to see you," Professor Paleo told him. "This is really exciting. Look we are unloading casts of some newly discovered dinosaur tracks."

"Can I come later," Terry replied. "I need to go to the workshop now."

"It will take just a minute," the professor told him as she pointed. "Look at these tracks. Most of these tracks were made by dinosaurs we are familiar with. See, here are some made by a diplodocus. These tracks were made by an ankylosaurus and those by a stegosaur. And here are tyrannosaur tracks.

But some of these tracks are really strange. These look as if they were made by a track type tractor like you, but we know that is impossible. I wonder what kind of dinosaur could have made them."

The boss said, "That's truly amazing."

Then the boss remembered what Terry had been saying about being with dinosaurs. He asked him, "Terry do you have any ideas about this mystery?"

But Terry only winked a headlight and said, "I think you might want to talk with Professor Portend. He might have a clue about these tracks."

TERRY'S DINO FRIENDS' SONG

Friends are where you find them. For friends are ev' ry- where in a sur- pris-ing place you'll find a new friend there

by SHERRY SECKLER

The Illustrator

Mike and Sabrina always come up with the most interesting challenges for me as an illustrator. Fortunately, they always provide lots of reference art for me to go by – in this case lots of dinosaur pictures.

This time Mike told me to make the dinosaurs look really stupid. I asked "How do I make a dinosaur look stupid?" Well, I tried and I hope they look stupid enough.

I just cannot believe that this is the seventeenth adventure of Terry the Tractor.

Author's comments

Sabrina has a great imagination. When I again told her that I had no plans for a new Terry the Tractor story she came back to me with the idea for this one. All kids like dinosaurs – and most kids like tractors – but this is the first book I know of that features both.

Kids seem to love the long strange names for various species of dinosaur. Just to make sure they can properly pronounce the ones featured in this book I have included a guide below.

Tyrannosaurus rex – Pronunciation: tie-RAN-oh-SORE-rus REX *Meaning of name:* king tyrant lizard

Diplodocus – Pronunciation: dye-PLOD-oh-kus *Meaning of name:* double beam (Because its head and tail stuck out like long beams)

Ankylosaurus – Pronunciation: ang-KILE-oh-SAW-rus *Meaning of name:* fused lizard (With the anatomical meaning: "stiff" or "fused")

Stegosaurus – Pronunciation: STEG-oh-SAW-rus *Meaning of name:* roof lizard (Because the plates on its back resemble a roof)

Books in the Terry the Tractor series
by Mike Rucker

Terry the Tractor
Terry and the Bully
Terry the Athlete
Terry and the Super Powerful Fuel
Terry and the Elephant
Terry and the Ecological Disaster
Terry and the High-Tech Laser Guided, Satellite Transmitted, Dozing System
Terry and the South Pole Breakdown
Terry the Smoke Jumper
Terry and the Wild Well Blowout
Terry and the Beaver Dam Fiasco
Terry and the Trouble with Trash
Terry and the Obsolete Locomotive
Terry and the Earthquake
Terry and the Martians
Terry and the Sunken Submarine
Terry and the Dinosaurs

Coming Soon:

Terry and the Future of the World

To order any of the Terry the Tractor books, send a check for $5.95 (includes postage) for each title to:

Mike Rucker
1003 W. Centennial Dr.
Peoria, IL 61614-2828

Or, visit Terry on the worldwide web at: **www.terrythetractor.com**